THE TOWER OF LONDON

PAST & PRESENT

GEOFFREY PARNELL

The History Press

An atmospheric photograph of the Tower from Southwark, *c.* 1880.

First published 1998
This edition first published 2009

The History Press
The Mill, Brimscombe Port
Stroud, Gloucestershire, GL5 2QG
www.thehistorypress.co.uk

British Library Cataloguing in Publication Data.
A catalogue record for this book is available from the British Library.

ISBN 978 0 7524 5036 0

Typesetting and origination by The History Press
Printed in Great Britain

CONTENTS

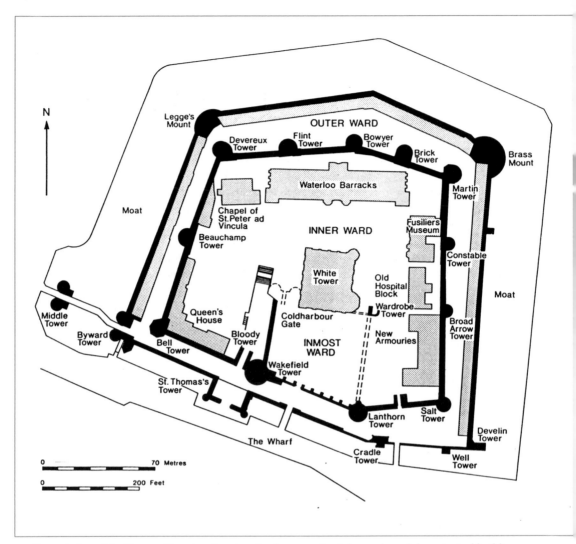

General plan of the Tower of London showing the three wards of the castle and the principal buildings.

INTRODUCTION

T he Tower of London occupies a special place in the history of the English nation and through this association has become one of the most famous buildings in the world. Popular images of ravens, Yeoman Warders, Crown Jewels and an almost unfathomable interest in the myth of a grim fortress-prison bring more than 2½ million visitors inside the castle's walls each year and an unknown number to view them from the outside.

The fortifications encompass an area of 12 acres (5 ha). Add to this the Wharf and the outlying Liberties (a strip of ground beyond the moat on the three landward sides of the castle, historically administered by the Tower authorities or their appointees) and the figure rises to 18 acres (7 ha). Not all this was laid out in one operation. Indeed the process took nearly 250 years, beginning in the winter of 1066/7 when, as William of Poitiers, William the Conqueror's biographer, put it, 'certain strongholds were made in the city against the fickleness of the vast and fierce population'. From the beginning, therefore, the Tower was as much a fortress to subdue the City as one to defend it.

View of the Tower from Tower Hill, *c.* 1850. This is the earliest known photograph of the fortress and was taken by Mr G. Hilditch, who entered it in an exhibition organised by the Royal Society of Arts in 1852.

Major Lewis Alexander Hall of the Royal
Engineers, who directed much of the Office of
Ordnance restoration programme at the Tower
during the 1840s.

The first Norman emergency enclosure comprised a ditch and earthen rampart laid out in the angle of
the old wall that protected the Roman city of Londinium. Occupying little more than 1 acre (0.5 ha) this
part of the castle, which contains the great White Tower, is referred to as the Inmost Ward. From an early
date there was probably an outer bailey, or enclosure, of some kind, but as yet we do not know whether
or not it was defended. It is not until Richard I came to the throne in 1189 that clear evidence for the
enlargement of the defences is forthcoming. In that year, and immediately after the King had embarked
on a crusade to the Holy Land, the chancellor, William Longchamp, began to erect, at considerable
expense, a new line of defence to the west of the Norman castle. Some of this work, the Bell Tower and
the adjoining curtain wall to the east, both originally washed by the Thames, survive as part of the inner
wall. The rest of the inner defences is largely the work of Henry III's masons, who around 1240–70 toiled,
with periodic interruptions, to create a vastly improved military stronghold in London to help control the
political intrigues and dissent of the King's barons. The area within the inner defences is called the Inner
Ward.

Finally, there is the Outer Ward, the narrow fortified corridor created by Edward I that surrounds the
castle. Built largely between the years 1275 and 1285, the enormous scale of the work is recorded in the
royal accounts with a combined expenditure of some £21,000, more than double what Edward's father,
Henry III, spent on the castle during his long reign. With the completion of the outer curtain wall and
the associated entrances the Tower had reached its ultimate expansion, thus gaining the concentric plan it
retains to this day.

The architectural development of the castle was far from over, however. Within the walls the Tower provided a secure environment to various official departments and institutions, and during the next 600 years these bodies constantly sought to improve their facilities, thereby creating an ever-changing landscape which bears little resemblance to the one that exists today.

By the end of the Middle Ages the Tower was not only a royal residence, but the home of the Royal Menagerie, the Record Office, the Mint, the Office of Ordnance (which supplied the armed forces with cannon, handguns and the more traditional bow and arrow), the Office of Armoury (which provided the same with armour and edged weapons) and the Wardrobe (which, apart from looking after the Crown Jewels, provided the royal household with soft furnishings, furniture, clothing and a host of other items). Add to this list the Constable of the Tower, his deputies and their households, the Body of Yeoman Warders and their families, state prisoners and their servants, and the occupants of a certain number of inns, and it is not difficult to imagine what a crowded, and potentially chaotic, community the Tower of London could present.

Nothing, as they say, remains the same and the seventeenth century saw the last royal occupation of the castle by James I, while the Wardrobe never really re-established itself after the depredations of England's first attempt at becoming a republic (i.e. the Commonwealth). Furthermore, developments in the art of war saw the demand for armour steadily decrease and thus, in 1671, the Office of Armoury was dissolved, and its stores and remaining functions passed to the ever-expanding Office of Ordnance.

More dramatic and far-reaching changes were to come in the nineteenth century, however, as many of the official occupants finally moved out of the Tower to more spacious accommodation elsewhere. The process began in 1812 when the Mint abandoned its facilities in the Outer Ward for a new building just outside the fortress on Little Tower Hill. The Menagerie closed in 1835 (after a lion was accused of biting a soldier) and its exotic occupants moved to Regent's Park Zoo. The Record Office withdrew from the Wakefield Tower and its adjoining chamber block, and from the White Tower during the 1850s. It was,

Anthony Salvin, the architect appointed to oversee the restoration of the Tower during the 1850s and '60s.

Sir John Taylor, the Office of Works architect who directed restorations at the Tower during the last three decades of the nineteenth century.

however, the gradual phasing out of the stores, workshops and offices of the War Office (which took over the responsibilities of the Office of Ordnance in 1855) that would bring about the vacation of the largest areas of the Tower. In the wake of these withdrawals, the Office of Works, the direct descendant of those who had directed the building of the castle for the medieval kings of England, undertook a major programme of 'restoration' to a fortress that was now regarded, first and foremost, as an ancient monument and tourist attraction. Since this great Victorian 'remedievalisation' of the fortress, alterations to the fabric have been much more tightly controlled in line with the concept of conservation, as opposed to re-creation, while the way in which the buildings and their contents are presented have changed to help the visitor better understand what he or she sees.

The Tower of London's transition from a complex of workshops and storehouses to an historic monument of the modern era represents perhaps the most radical change the castle has ever experienced. It would be fair to say, however, that until recently the episode has not received a great deal of attention. This is almost entirely because most authors have been preoccupied with the Crown Jewels and the state prisoners. Much of what is written is romantic and poorly researched and often simply perpetuates the myths and mistakes of earlier published accounts. In this respect the story of the Tower from the mid-nineteenth century has one unique record that is not so easily distorted or misinterpreted – that is the record of the photographer. The camera can, and does, provide dramatic images of the past for all to read, and the Tower of London is, after all, one of the most photographed buildings in the world. It is surprising, therefore, that no study of the historic photography of the fortress has been published before. I trust this modest effort helps to fill the gap.

Dr Geoffrey Parnell
Royal Armouries
HM Tower of London
3 December 1997

CHAPTER ONE

THE BUILDINGS

T he great changes that shaped the Tower of London we see today began with the burning of the seventeenth-century Grand Storehouse, immediately north of the White Tower, on the evening of 30 October 1841. On the cleared site of the storehouse in 1845 the Office of Ordnance, under the supervision of Major Lewis Alexander Hall of the Royal Engineers, began to build the existing Waterloo Barracks in a medieval gothic style. At the same time the badly damaged defensive walls and towers behind the new barracks were recast and a pair of large houses to the south-east (the present Royal Fusiliers Museum) extensively rebuilt as the officers' lodgings and mess. All this was completed in time to be captured on the earliest known photograph of the Tower, taken in about 1850.

Beginning in 1852, the restoration of the Tower, by now the responsibility of the Office of Works, was supervised by the eminent Victorian architect Anthony Salvin. By 1870 Salvin had completed major repairs and alterations to the Beauchamp Tower, Salt Tower, White Tower, St Thomas's Tower and Wakefield Tower (in that order). In addition he had produced the external design for the casemates (bomb-proof buildings) built in the 1850s and '60s along the north-east and east sides of the outer curtain wall, and had designed and supervised the building of the Pump House at the western entrance to the Tower and the pair of Tudor-style houses immediately west of the Bloody Tower, facing Tower Green. The latter were intended for Yeoman Warders and their families and represent Salvin's last commission at the Tower.

Throughout the remainder of the nineteenth century, restoration work was directed by the Office of Works architect, John Taylor, who was subsequently knighted for this and other projects he was concerned with. Taylor exercised a very thorough approach to 'restoration' or re-creation and under his supervision many historically important buildings were pulled down or needlessly altered, simply because they did not comply with an aesthetic idea of what a medieval castle should look like. Some of the worst excesses were associated with the clearance of the Inmost Ward and the 'reconstruction' of the inner defences between the Salt and Wakefield towers in 1879–88. We can only lament that any of this vandalism was allowed to take place, especially when a wiser and more conservation-minded approach to historic architecture was taking hold elsewhere.

That said, a genuine appreciation of old buildings was ultimately enhanced by the sense of loss that the exploits of people like Taylor at the Tower engendered: 'the darkest hour always precedes the dawn'. However, even today, and with our historic building legislation, we should remain vigilant and not assume that the fabric of places like the Tower of London is free from the dangers associated with aesthetic taste and commercial exploitation.

The Tower's buildings are, of course, part of the principal exhibition, and the way that they have been presented to the visitor over the years is a fascinating subject in its own right. Eighteenth-century guidebooks may be peppered with anecdotal comments about historic characters and events, but on the whole their authors do not appear to have been too concerned with attributing such information to precise buildings and places. In the nineteenth century, and with the rise of the Romantic Movement, however, all that was to change. Increasingly visitors came to the Tower expecting to see the masonry and relics that comprised the drama of history. Since most of the relevant material had long since disappeared, the hacks and tour guides of the day began to invent on a grand scale.

The Queen's House, for example, the only remaining sixteenth-century building in the fortress, was rapidly associated with every notable Tudor prisoner that had passed through the Tower – including Anne Boleyn, whose 'bedroom' is notable for being in existence four years before the house was built! Meanwhile, a short distance away, the Council Chamber, created in 1607 by the insertion of a mezzanine floor into the former great hall, became the unquestioned setting for the examination of Guy Fawkes in 1605. Worse still, the peg-holes in the roof timbers overhead, vacated by the removal of the bracing in 1607, became fixings that prisoners were hanged from during the act of torture! Such nonsense may be the stuff that historic yarns are made of, but how much more meaningful and beneficial it is to appreciate old buildings for what they are, rather than what wild imaginations would have them.

The Tower viewed from Tower Hill, *c.* 1880.

The view in 1997. The trees in the moat gardens have matured and a one-way system permits traffic up the Hill only.

The western entrance to the Tower photographed by James Davies Burton in 1868 with the Middle
Tower nearest to the camera. This stereoscopic photocard was made about ten years after the old
menagerie buildings in front of the Middle Tower had been pulled down and the area landscaped and
planted with trees. Note the presence of the Wharf Guard immediately to the south (right) of the Byward
Tower. This was the last of a sequence of guard-houses to occupy the site from Tudor times.

The view now includes one of the most remarkable bridges in the world – Tower Bridge, which was formally opened on 30 June 1894.

The western entrance to the Tower viewed from the Wharf in 1934. The long, single-storeyed building was designed in 1851 as a purpose-built ticket office, with toilets and refreshment room incorporated.

Sadly the ticket office was demolished in 1935 when the former Victorian Pump House, the building on the left, was extended northwards to form a ground floor restaurant with offices above. This photograph, taken in June 1935, shows work in progress. At this stage the northern half of the old office is still standing and in use, while the dispensing of refreshments has transferred to a temporary tent.

The view in 1997, with the unprepossessing 1960s Bowring Building in the background.

The steam engine in the Pump House at the western entrance, *c.* 1870. The Pump House was built in 1866 to replace an earlier arrangement beneath St Thomas's Tower, where Thames water for drinking and for fire fighting had been pumped into giant cisterns on top of the White Tower. The engine room in the photograph now forms part of the Tower Shop.

The Byward Tower, part of Edward I's great western approach to the castle, photographed by James Davies Burton in 1868.

Apart from the loss of the chimney stacks and a lot of surface grime the view today has altered little.

The Byward Tower and causeway, pictured from the Wharf, *c.* 1880. The building partly covered in ivy to the right of the picture is the Byward Barbican, a fifteenth-century gun tower which guarded the bridge over the moat at this point. This crossing was the principal entrance into the castle for important visitors arriving by boat until the nineteenth century.

The view in 1997 shows the Yeoman Warders' bowling green now occupying the site of the Victorian vegetable allotments in the moat.

A late nineteenth-century photograph of the rear of Byward Tower with a glimpse of the old Yeoman Warders' Hall on the left. Seventeenth-century plans and documents make it clear that the name Byward derives from 'By Warders', a reference to the Warders' Hall next to the tower.

Between 1925 and 1929 various post-medieval additions to the gatehouse were removed to reveal, as the jargon goes, 'a wealth of exposed timbers'. The effect may be picturesque but, historically, is quite misleading, as most of the timberwork was never intended to be seen. The Warders' Hall also suffered from a thorough refacing during the 1920s and now serves as an information point.

One of the most popular views of the Tower, with the Bloody and Wakefield towers on the left-hand side of Water Lane, and St Thomas's Tower on the right. This photograph was taken in about 1880, before the early eighteenth-century windows in the Bloody Tower were replaced.

The view in 1997.

(*Above*) A photograph taken by Benjamin Stone in 1898 showing the ground floor of the Wakefield Tower. The brick vault was inserted in 1867–8 by Anthony Salvin to support the re-display of the Crown Jewels on the first floor.

The same view after the restoration of the Wakefield Tower was completed in 1971, and showing the timber floor that was reinstated on the documentary and archaeological evidence for the original early thirteenth-century structure.

The Wakefield Tower and adjoining Record Office, with its ornate entrance surmounted by the royal arms, *c.* 1880. The carcass of the Record Office originally formed part of the private apartments erected for Henry III in the early thirteenth century. By the reign of Henry VIII it had become a depository for state papers and remained so until the mid-nineteenth century.

Despite a spirited campaign by the Society for the Protection of Ancient Buildings the Record Office was demolished in 1885.

The Bloody Tower and the Main Guard, photographed by H. W. Field in the early 1860s. The Main Guard was formed in 1846 around the shell of an earlier storehouse, which itself incorporated Henry III's inner curtain wall.

The view is quite different 130 years later. The Main Guard was pulled down in 1898 to make way for another guard-house, which in turn was demolished in 1944, when the remains of the medieval curtain wall were revealed. Alterations have also taken place to the Bloody Tower, including the renewal of the upper window, which was probably installed in 1605–6 for the benefit of Sir Walter Ralegh.

The Main Guard erected between 1898 and 1900, immediately to the north of the Wakefield Tower, on the site of the earlier guard-house. This large brick structure, sometimes referred to as Queen Victoria's Canteen, contained in addition to the guard room an orderly room, office, stores, a recreation area, mess and lecture rooms. It was the last major building to be erected at the Tower in the Victorian gothic tradition, and is pictured here shortly after it was gutted by fire in October 1940.

The view in 1997, showing the remains of Henry III's curtain wall which was exposed during demolition of the Main Guard in 1944.

The eastern annex to the White Tower shortly before its demolition in 1879. Thought to have originated as Edward III's wardrobe, the south-east corner of the building (nearest to the camera) incorporated the twelfth-century Wardrobe Tower, part of which appeared to be standing to its full height when this picture was taken.

Unfortunately much of what remained of the Wardrobe Tower was lost during demolition of the annex, before antiquarians were able to intervene to save what we see today.

The crenellated New Horse Armoury, built in 1825 against the south side of the White Tower, pictured during the course of its demolition in 1883. Note the early medieval wall linking the apse of the White Tower to the remains of the Wardrobe Tower. This intriguing feature was removed as part of an obsessive campaign to rid the White Tower of its appendages during the 1880s.

It seems, however, that the White Tower can never be free of additions, as demonstrated by the scaffolding seen here in 1997.

A photograph of about 1895 showing the summit of the north-east turret of the White Tower, which was fitted out as a clock tower in 1853–4. The first Astronomer Royal, John Flamsteed, carried out observations from the top of this tower (known as Flamsteed's Tower) between April and July 1675, before his departure to the new observatory at Greenwich.

In 1913 the clock mechanism and clock faces were removed and the masonry restored to the condition we see today.

The Chapel of St John in the White Tower, *c.* 1880. The finest Norman interior in the White Tower, the Chapel served as a record office from at least the end of the sixteenth century until the 1850s. In 1864 it was restored by Anthony Salvin, and some years later dissenters were allowed to worship there. The communion table seen here was installed for their benefit in 1878.

The Chapel after its refurbishment in 1967.

A late nineteenth-century photograph of the
doorway in the basement of the White Tower
connecting the east chamber and the sub-crypt.
The original Norman wall passage was probably
enlarged in the middle of the fourteenth
century, the date to which the existing oak
panelled door has been scientifically assigned.
At the time this photograph was taken the
passage was erroneously identified as 'Little
Ease', a small prison cell mentioned several
times in the sixteenth century, the location of
which is not known.

A late nineteenth-century photograph of the sub-crypt in the basement of the White Tower. This had been
a gunpowder store throughout most of the eighteenth and nineteenth centuries, but by the time this
photograph was taken it was more dramatically identified as the 'Great Dungeon'.

The Queen's House, the L-shaped official residence of the Governor of the Tower of London, in the south-west corner of the Inner Ward. It was built in 1540 and incorporated the remains of the fourteenth-century Constable's House. This view, taken in about 1870, shows the building from the east.

The same view in 1997, showing the building without the plasterwork and other accretions that were removed in 1915.

The south range of the Queen's House in 1914.

The same view taken the following year and after the timber frame had been exposed. Note the seventeenth-century stair turret on the left of the picture. This interesting addition to the original Tudor building was taken down in 1960.

The wall-walk along the inner curtain leading to the Bell Tower, *c.* 1870. In the nineteenth century it was said that Queen Elizabeth I was lodged in the Bell Tower, so the wall-walk was duly named Elizabeth's Walk. In practice it would have been a lapse of protocol to have lodged a member of the royal family in such spartan surroundings, and there is no reason to suppose that Elizabeth was not provided with chambers in the royal lodgings near the Lanthorn Tower, which in the eighteenth century was still referred to as 'Queen Elizabeth's Tower'.

The view along the wall-walk today, showing the re-created crenellations that were introduced at the turn of the century.

A photograph of 4 and 5 Tower Green in 1922. A pair of mid-seventeenth-century domestic houses, they were perhaps originally occupied by servants of the Lieutenant of the Tower who, until the eighteenth century, lived in the adjoining Queen's House.

In 1922, when the houses were underpinned to prevent subsidence, the opportunity was taken to remove a layer of nineteenth-century render from the external brickwork.

(Above) The interior of the first floor of the Beauchamp Tower, *c.* 1880. The building was restored by Anthony Salvin in 1852–3 and this chamber was opened to the public shortly thereafter so that visitors could see the numerous and well-preserved prisoners' inscriptions that line the walls. The handrail deterred visitors from getting too close to the walls and touching the carvings.

The John Dudley inscription, one of the most elaborate and accomplished carvings to be found in the Beauchamp Tower, reproduced in a stereoscopic card of about 1870. The device, featuring the beasts of the Warwick badge, was cut during the imprisonment of Dudley and his sons in 1553-4. Beneath is an anonymous depiction of a man kneeling at an alter.

A photograph taken in about 1880 of 1 and 2 Tower Green, located immediately north of the Beauchamp Tower. No. 1 (to the right) has been the site of the residence of the Tower Chaplain since at least 1616. The house pictured here dates from 1749. No. 2 was built in 1735 for a clerk of the Office of Ordnance, but by the time this picture was taken it had become the official residence of the Tower medical officer – a post that also goes back many centuries.

Nos 1 and 2 Tower Green as they appear today, still occupied by the Tower Chaplain and Doctor.

The Chapel of St Peter ad Vincula. Probably originating as a Saxon city church, it stood outside the walls of the castle proper until the reign of Henry III. Henry III greatly embellished the church, but Edward I had it rebuilt in 1286–7. The structure that exists now dates essentially from 1510–20, when it was rebuilt following a fire. This early photograph shows the building with its Tudor porch, which was removed in 1862.

The Chapel as it appears today, after further renovations were carried out in the early 1970s.

The east end of the Chapel of St Peter ad Vincula, *c.* 1870. The pedimented reredos and altar rails were installed in 1675–6 as part of a general refurbishment of the Chapel during the reign of Charles II. The box pews, with their candle holders, were added in the eighteenth century for the benefit of the garrison.

A photograph taken during the 1920s, showing the stone altar, pulpit and wooden benches installed in 1876–7 as part of the restoration of the Chapel.

The view today, showing the altar and furniture installed in the early 1970s.

The great martial arms carved by John Young for the Grand Storehouse in 1691 mounted on a wall near the Martin Tower in about 1870. They were placed here a few years after fire destroyed the storehouse in 1841. Behind the arms, and to the right, may be seen the New Jewel House of 1840–1.

The view in 1997 has changed significantly. John Young's carving was moved inside the New Armouries in 1976 to protect the stonework from the adverse effects of the weather, while the Jewel House was demolished after the Jewels were transferred to the Wakefield Tower in 1870.

A stereoscopic view showing the Martin Tower and part of the adjoining New Jewel House taken by James Davies Burton in 1868. The tower at this time formed the residence of the Jewel Keeper, who may be seen with his wife by the main entrance to the building.

The view in 1997, showing the various alterations that have taken place since the late nineteenth century.

The Officers' Mess near the north-east corner of the White Tower, *c.* 1880. This was built to complement the Waterloo Barracks in the second half of the 1840s. Parts of the fabric, however, seem to include the remains of a pair of great houses built for the Surveyor and Clerk of the Ordnance in 1699–1701.

The building in 1997, now housing the Royal Fusiliers Museum. This regiment was first raised at the Tower in 1685.

The New Armouries during the 1920s. This interesting brick storehouse was built in 1663–4 as a store for small arms. Between 1688 and 1825 the first floor was home to the Line of Kings – a display of mounted figures representing the Kings of England which, until 1883, was one of the Tower's most popular visitor attractions.

The New Armouries in 1997. In 1947 the building was transferred to the Tower Armouries and converted into museum galleries and offices (hence its name). At that time, and subsequently, it suffered a series of 'improvements' which sought to conceal the building's origins by 'Georgianising' its appearance.

(*Above*) The rear of the Cradle Tower taken in 1879 after the reinstatement of the upper floor. The original floor was removed in 1776 in advance of the construction of the Ordnance office, whose south-east corner may be seen on the left of the picture. The Cradle Tower was built between 1348 and 1355 as a private water-gate for Edward III. Its construction was evidently interrupted and delayed by the Black Death.

The view today no longer includes the former Ordnance office or the original warehouses around St Katherine's Dock in the background.

A view of the partly reconstructed Cradle Tower taken from the Wharf in 1879. Beyond the Cradle Tower may be seen the Well Tower which, together with the intervening curtain wall and East Drawbridge, were all heavily restored in 1878–9.

The view today, with the reconstructed St Katherine's Dock warehouses in the background.

The Constable Tower on the inner eastern curtain wall photographed after its virtual reconstruction in 1849–50. The view formed part of a remarkable set of stereoscopic cards issued by Henry Dages and Alfred Harman in 1861, which provided the first comprehensive photographic study of the buildings of the Tower. In the foreground may be seen the remains of an extension to the Irish Barracks, erected in 1805, and beyond the New Jewel House of 1840–1.

The view today without the nineteenth-century buildings.

The East Drawbridge viewed from the Wharf in about 1870. An opening in the curtain wall was forced through this point in 1774 and embellished in a classical manner. The gateway pictured here is a replacement, the original having been reformed not long before this photograph was taken.

The gateway we see today dates from the restoration of the river defences in 1878–9. The drawbridge itself is now a fixed structure of a later date.

A view of St Thomas's Tower taken by Henry and Alfred Harman in 1861 and before the partial collapse of the south-east turret in June 1862. This remarkable view shows the windows introduced by the masonry contractor Andrews Jelfe in 1735 when the upper floor served as the Tower Infirmary.

ST. THOMAS'S TOWER.

The same view reproduced and embellished as an engraving in a new guide to the Tower published in 1863. Note the tarpaulin in front of Traitors' Gate, intended to provide privacy for soldiers of the garrison who used the water-filled basin beneath the building as a sort of large bathing pool!

The formidable row of buildings that occupied the line of the inner defences, 1882. From left to right these include the Wakefield Tower, the Record Office, the 'D-Stores' and the former Ordnance office. In the foreground may be seen the opening made through the outer curtain wall in 1834 for the Middle Drawbridge crossing.

The view today bears little resemblance.

The former Ordnance office seen rising above the river defences in 1882. Built in two phases between 1777 and 1792, this once lavishly decorated building was converted into a storehouse and given an upper floor during the Crimean War (1853–6). The heightening obscured the view of the White Tower and did nothing to enhance the architectural quality of the building. In 1866 Lord de Ros, Lieutenant of the Tower, described it as having the 'decorative style of the great gin-palaces of London'.

The view today, showing John Taylor's reconstructed defences.

The Drill Battery at the eastern end of the Wharf, *c.* 1890. Heavy guns were placed here during the 1860s, at a time when fortifications were being erected at strategic locations in the British Isles to guard against a possible French invasion.

In 1997 three guns provide the only echo of the once formidable battery, while closer to the Tower the Victorian lawn is now extensively occupied by an unprepossessing cafeteria.

A general view of the Tower from Southwark on the south side of the river, *c.* 1880. This photograph demonstrates just how busy the Thames waterway was at that time.

The view today is deserted by comparison.

CHAPTER TWO

THE DISPLAYS

By Tudor times the Tower of London was already regarded as a supreme ancient monument. It was associated with a great deal of dramatic English history and many of its buildings and spaces were linked to betrayal, treason and the fall from power. In addition it had always been a great storehouse and there are references dating back to the Middle Ages of important visitors coming to the fortress to view the armoury. It is, however, from the end of Elizabeth I's reign that evidence appears for less exalted, but fee-paying, visitors coming to see the attractions. One of the earliest was Joseph Platter, a Swiss traveller from Basle, who paid 21s for the privilege of viewing the armoury in the White Tower in 1599.

The emergence of themed arms displays specifically designed to entertain and intrigue the visitor seems to date from the reign of Charles II. The earliest were the Line of Kings and the Spanish Armoury. The former, as the name suggests, was a row of figures representing the Kings of England. They appeared on life-size wooden horses wearing what were claimed to be their personal armours. The second collection, the Spanish Armoury, comprised a group of fearsome-looking weapons, and a few instruments of torture, that were said to have been taken from the disastrous Armada of 1588. In 1696 a third display, the Small Armoury, was set up on the first floor of the Grand Storehouse on the hill behind the White Tower. This was by far the most spectacular of the Tower displays and comprised some 60,000 weapons and a mass of elaborate carvings arranged together into such wonderfully eccentric figures as a fiery serpent, a seven-headed monster, the waves of the sea, the backbones of a whale, a giant organ and the 'Witch of Endor'.

Within a few years the hall beneath the Small Armoury had also become a visitor attraction. Called the Artillery Room, this not only contained the great guns of the armed forces, but increasingly guns and other trophies captured from battlefields around the world together with certain domestic items of historic curiosity. By 1708 these included that most infamous, but by then long de-commissioned, of Tower objects, the 'Rack of Torment'.

During the nineteenth century the Tower Armouries underwent a radical transformation. In 1826 the Line of Kings was transferred to a specially constructed building against the south side of the White Tower known as the New Horse Armoury. This was one of the earliest public museums to be built in the country, though it was criticised on architectural grounds. A commentator in the *Builder* magazine, for example, expressed his opinion that the 'perpetrator' of the design 'deserved to be beheaded'. Inside the building, and under the supervision of the great armour expert, Samuel Meyrick, the Line of Kings was rearranged in a more scientific manner, with some of the more glaring mistakes (such as a musket attributed to William the Conqueror!) being removed.

In 1831 the Spanish Armoury was officially renamed 'Queen Elizabeth's Armoury' and in 1837 it was transferred into the Crypt of the White Tower. In 1841 the burning of the Grand Storehouse resulted in the complete loss of the Small Armoury and many of the exhibits in the Artillery Room, sadly before any of these could be recorded by the camera. The following year the Crown Jewels were re-displayed in a new Jewel House erected against the south side of the Martin Tower. The new building was plagued by defects, however, and after various unsuccessful attempts had been made to improve the situation the Regalia were moved again in 1870, this time into the upper chamber of the Wakefield Tower where they remained until the 1960s.

After the restoration of the White Tower was completed in 1863, the first and second floors became home to thousands of rifles for the Volunteers, the equivalent of today's Territorial Army. Though a working arsenal, the rifles were racked in a very ornamental manner, and together with arrangements of armour and ancient weapons were viewed by the visiting public. These fantastic compositions were replaced in 1883 when the New Horse Armoury was demolished and its contents transferred into the White Tower. The remainder of the White Tower was vacated by the War Office and given over to the Tower Armouries during the early twentieth century – the ground floor in 1914, the basement in 1916. Since then the displays in the building have been rearranged on a number of occasions.

The so-called scaffold site in front of the Chapel of St. Peter ad Vincula photographed by James Davies Burton in 1868. In fact, the site was only invented four years earlier following a royal visit to the Tower in July 1861, during which Prince Albert informed the Lieutenant-Governor of Queen's Victoria's desire to see the spot where Anne Boleyn was beheaded marked with a stone and inscription. Contemporary Tudor accounts, however, make it clear that the event actually took place to the east on ground between the White Tower and the present Waterloo Barracks.

One of the earliest known stereoscopic views of the Tower published by Negretti & Zambra in 1859, showing a statue of the Duke of Wellington on the Parade Ground in front of the Waterloo Barracks. The statue was sculpted by Thomas Milnes and unveiled in December 1848 as a compliment to the newly constructed barracks bearing the name of the Duke's great victory over the French. The work was not universally acclaimed, however, and after being described as 'poor and pompous' was moved to Woolwich Arsenal in 1863, where it remains to this day.

The view today without the statue, but supplemented by the clock over the entrance to the barracks added in 1913.

(*Above*) A stereoscopic view of the so-called Gun Park on the west side of the White Tower in the 1860s. Historic guns rescued from the ruins of the Grand Storehouse were first placed here in 1841. In default of any other suitable accommodation, the site continued to act as a store for large guns until the early twentieth century. The stone pedestal behind the soldier was the base for a statue of the Duke of Wellington that was transferred to Woolwich in 1863.

Another early stereoscopic view of the Gun Park looking north and with the Waterloo Barracks in the background.

A stereoscopic postcard of the 1860s showing the interior of the New Horse Armoury looking east. The Line of Kings is on the left.

(Opposite) The interior of the New Horse Armoury looking west, *c.* 1870.

Another mounted figure of Henry VIII wearing the formidable armour made for him at Greenwich in 1540. This photograph was also taken in the New Horse Armoury in about 1870.

A photograph of about 1870 showing the figure of James II in the Line of Kings, wearing the armour made for him by Richard Hoden of London in 1686.

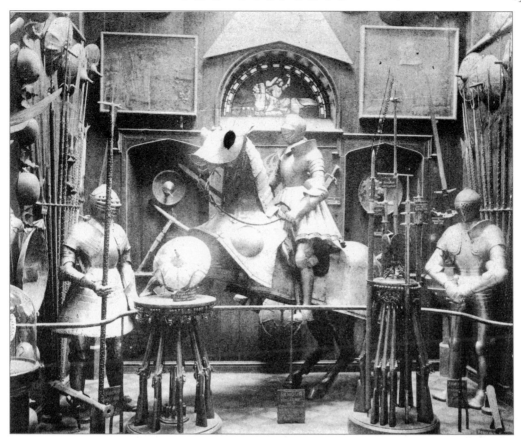

One of the figures of Henry VIII in the Line of Kings, wearing his famous silvered and engraved armour which celebrated the King's union with Catherine of Aragon. It is seen here in the New Horse Armoury in about 1870.

This stereoscopic card, issued by Frank Good in about 1870, includes the earliest known view of the 'Executioner's Mask' (to the right of the shield) a nineteenth-century piece of fakery that visitors were told was worn by the 'Executioner of the Tower'. At this time the mask was mounted on a wall of the Eastern Vestibule of the New Horse Armoury.

A photograph taken in about 1870 showing one of the many trophy displays that decorated the walls of the New Horse Armoury. This star is composed of swords, scabbards and pistols. Note also the glazed window – part of the collection of painted glass obtained in 1842 from Strawberry Hill, Twickenham, the famous Gothic home of Horace Walpole. Remnants of the glass may now be seen in the windows of the Chapel of St John in the White Tower.

A view of Queen Elizabeth's Armoury in the Crypt of the White Tower, *c.* 1870. Originally called the Spanish Armoury, the display was moved into the Crypt in 1831. Six years later it was reformed and renamed Queen Elizabeth's Armoury, at which time the elegant columns and ceiling ribs were added. The display comprised a heady mixture of myth and imagination and included a collection of fearsome-looking weapons, instruments of torture – some historic Tower display items, others recently purchased or manufactured fakes – and the block and axe (seen in the foreground).

These figures of Queen Elizabeth I and her page were made by Benjamin Wilson at the outbreak of the war with Spain in 1779. The horse is earlier, probably the beast made by Grinling Gibbons in 1685 for the figure of Charles II in the Line of Kings. The group is seen here at the west end of Queen Elizabeth's Armoury in about 1870.

The uppermost eastern chamber of the White Tower in about 1870, showing part of the Volunteers Armoury. Thousands of rifles on this floor and in the two great chambers below were arranged into gigantic columns. In this picture you can also see one of the enormous gas lamps known as 'wedding cakes' that were made out of weapons and weapon parts. Natural light was provided by skylights in the roof and light wells in the floors surrounded by barriers made from swords.

A view from the uppermost eastern chamber of the White Tower into the adjoining western chamber in about 1870, showing rifle columns interspersed with patterns of ancient arms and armour. In addition to seating, the visiting public were provided with information about the compositions on ornate wooden shields.

A view along one of the passages in the thickness of the wall of the White Tower at the level of the uppermost floor, c. 1870. Once again large numbers of weapons were deployed to create architectural features such as panelling.

The view along the deserted passage today.

A view of part of the great western chamber on the first floor of the White Tower taken during the 1870s. The installation of the Volunteers Armoury was completed in 1863 and in addition to the thousands of serviceable rifles that the visiting public could inspect were displays of historic armour and ingenious devices composed of weapon parts. Here, on the left of the picture, and made of sword blades, may be seen the leaves and flower of a plant trained against the sides of a window opening.

(Opposite above) A late nineteenth-century photograph of the Armouries in the uppermost western chamber of the White Tower. These displays replaced the Volunteers Arsenal in 1883, most of the exhibits having come from the New Horse Armoury, which was demolished in that year.

(Opposite below) A photograph of the great western chamber on the first floor of the White Tower at the end of the nineteenth century. Note the elaborate ceiling displays which include ammunition belts snaking along the sides of the light wells.

The view along the north end of the uppermost western chamber of the White Tower at the end of the nineteenth century. Amidst this marvellous jumble of exhibits are the figures of Queen Elizabeth and her page, recently transferred from the Crypt on the first floor below.

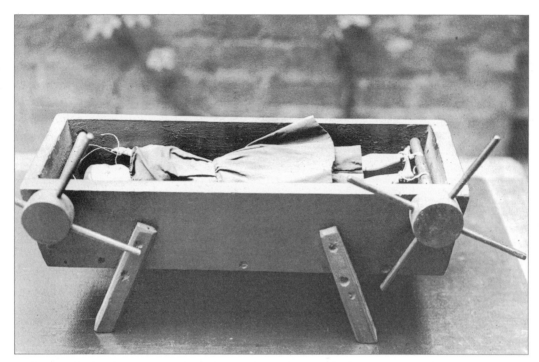

A photograph taken by Benjamin Stone in 1898 of a miniature rack, one of several made for display in the Tower during the second half of the nineteenth century. Women are depicted on all the devices, perhaps indicating an unhealthy fascination with the only recorded racking of a woman, Anne Askew, in 1546.

This late nineteenth-century photograph shows how the Crown Jewels were displayed in a glass case behind railings.

The Crown Jewels in the upper chamber of the Wakefield Tower, *c.* 1905. The great cage was made by Messrs Brown & Downing, iron founders of Birmingham, in 1869. The mesh was added at a later date to improve security.

In 1910–11 the security of the Crown Jewels in the Wakefield Tower was again improved. Among the measures taken was the replacement of the Victorian case and railings with the daunting device illustrated here. It remained in use until the Regalia were moved to a new Jewel House in 1967.

CHAPTER THREE

THE WORLD WARS

The two great wars of the twentieth century affected both the life and the fabric of the Tower. Throughout the First World War the castle remained open to the public, though visits were sometimes disrupted by a new and terrifying feature of modern warfare – the air raid. At the start of the war the Kaiser had specifically instructed his military commanders not to target the royal palaces and historic monuments of London. As the war dragged on, however, and air raids increased and targets became more diverse, the threat to the Tower of London grew. The basement of the White Tower and the old munitions tunnel that had once connected it to the Wharf were designated air raid shelters for residents and visitors alike. During one of the heaviest raids on London, on 13 June 1917, a bomb landed in the moat near Legge's Mount. It failed to explode and the only reported casualties were two pigeons. However, the Tower did suffer shrapnel damage during this and other raids. One of the more notable incidents of damage – to an ancillary building in the Outer Ward close to the Bowyer Tower – was not inflicted by an enemy bomb, but evidently by a spent projectile fired from an anti-aircraft gun planted on Tower Bridge! This gun position was for a time commanded by Charles ffoulkes, Curator of the Tower Armouries, and the gun crew attracted much public admiration when, on 19 May 1918, they managed to shoot down a Gotha bomber – probably the only occasion during the war when an enemy plane operating over London was brought down in this manner.

During the First World War the Tower staged something of a revival as a state prison and place of execution. Eleven German spies were executed in the fortress between November 1914 and April 1916. Some were shot by firing squad in the moat, others met the same fate in the Miniature Rifle Range. The most celebrated prisoner of the time was not a German, however, but the Irishman Roger Casement, who, having been found guilty of treason, was executed at Pentonville Prison on 3 August 1916.

The Second World War saw the Tower officially designated as a Prisoner of War Collection Centre. About 180 men in all passed through the fortress on their way to concentration camps in the north of England. Most were U-boat crewmen and Luftwaffe airmen. There were, however, two more exotic captives – Dr Herr Gerlach, the German Consul-General to Iceland, brought to the Tower for three-and- a-half months in June 1940, and Rudolf Hess, the Deputy Führer of Germany, who was held in the Queen's House for four days during May the following year. The role of the Tower as a state prison finally came to an end on 14 August 1941 when the convicted German spy Josef Jakobs was executed by firing squad in the Miniature Rifle Range.

Aerial bombardment caused considerable damage to the fabric of the Tower during the Second World War, notably between September and November 1940 when raids on the capital were at their most intense. In total some fifteen high-explosive bombs and innumerable incendiaries fell on and in the precincts of the fortress and three flying bombs exploded beside it. Several structures were blown apart or gutted by fire, while every building sustained damage of one sort or another. In advance of this onslaught the Crown Jewels and other treasures were evacuated, the former to a location that has never been disclosed. Public admission was suspended at the outbreak of hostilities, though privilege tours for Dominion and Allied troops were organised. When the agony of war ended, a battered and scarred Tower of London still stood. But it had been a narrow escape.

(Opposite above) The 2nd Scots Guards preparing to leave the Tower on the morning of 15 September 1914 for camp at Lyndhurst, in the New Forest, where the 7th Division was forming.

(Opposite below) The 2nd Scots Guards march down Water Lane on their way out of the Tower on 15 September 1914.

Smoke from the burning docks of East London provides a dramatic backdrop for Tower Bridge and the White Tower (far left) during the early evening of 7 September 1940, the day the Luftwaffe began its massive night bombing of London.

Opposite above) The Miniature Rifle Range, erected in the second half of 1915 in the Outer Ward between the Constable and Martin towers, was the venue for the execution of several German spies during the First World War and Josef Jacobs, a Sergeant in the German Army, on 14 August 1941.

(Opposite below) The site of the Rifle Range today. The shed was demolished in May 1969 only to be replaced by another mean structure in the form of a car port.

The North Bastion was built mid-way along the outer northern curtain wall at the time of the Chartist riots in the 1840s. This photograph shows just how close to the building an enemy bomb landed on the night of 10/11 September 1940.

On 5 October 1940 the North Bastion was blown apart by a high-explosive bomb. Sadly the occupant, Yeoman Warder Reeves, lost his life during the incident.

The former eighteenth-century Master of the Assay Office in the western Outer Ward. One of the few remaining buildings of the Royal Mint at the Tower, it was reduced to rubble by a high-explosive bomb on 23 September 1940.

The building was rebuilt in replica form after the end of the war.

At the outbreak of the war, the Old Hospital Block, built originally in 1718–19 as houses for Ordnance clerks and converted into accommodation for war invalids during the Crimean War, was surrounded by barbed wire and used to house German prisoners of war. The last inmates were removed in May 1940, thus avoiding the irony of being killed or injured by one of their own bombs, which partly demolished the terrace on 23 September 1940.

(*Opposite above*) In 1950 another part of the Old Hospital Block had to be demolished after the masonry was found to be structurally unsound.

(*Opposite below*) The partly reconstructed terrace as it appears today.

The Main Guard of 1898–1900, lying close to the south-west corner of the White Tower, was burnt out on the night of 29 December 1940 after fifty incendiary devices landed in the precincts of the Tower. A valiant effort was made to save the building, but strong winds and a lack of water pressure sealed its fate.

The view of the site of the Main Guard in 1997.

Another view of the gutted Main Guard
from the north-west in 1943.

Iron trusses were all that remained of the
roof of the Main Guard after the fire of
29 December 1940.

The munitions tunnel built from the Wharf to the south-west corner of the White Tower in 1834 is pictured here after being severely damaged by a bomb on 1 October 1940. The southern end of the tunnel was repaired, and for many years after the war served as a garage for the Resident Governor.

After a break of several hundred years the White Tower was again occupied by military personnel, during the Second World War. This photograph shows the great uppermost western chamber used as badminton court and theatre.

The adjoining uppermost eastern chamber served as a bar.

On the ground floor of the White Tower the eastern chamber was fitted out as a canteen and library.

The basement of the White Tower became an air raid shelter and also provided sleeping accommodation for the fire picket.

The inaugural raising of the barrage balloon in 1940 attracted a large crowd of onlookers.

(Opposite below) On 29 September 1940 a Royal Air Force detachment brought a barrage balloon to the Tower and tethered it to a position near the Byward Tower in the west moat. During the second half of the war the balloon was managed by a Women's Royal Air Force detachment who lived in huts in the moat.

During the war much of the moat was converted into vegetable allotments by the residents of the Tower.

One of the last defensive additions to the Tower of London was this Second World War pillbox. It stood at the eastern end of the Wharf and is pictured here shortly before demolition in 1959.

Labelled 'A "Beefeater" in his wartime disguise' this officially sanctioned photograph shows a Yeoman Warder equipped with steel helmet and gas mask.

(*Above*) The streets around the Tower of London suffered terrible damage during the Blitz. This photograph, taken from the parapet of the Church of All Hallows Barking shows the situation on Tower Hill. A cluster of buildings, including the Tiger Tavern, an inn with long associations with the Tower, remain standing near the castle's western entrance. Having survived the onslaught of the German air force, these buildings were demolished in the 1960s to make way for the unmemorable glass and concrete office complex called the Bowring Building.

The Tower of London reopened to the public on 1 January 1946. This photograph records the return of tourists to a landmark still scarred by the effects of war.

CHAPTER FOUR

COMMUNITY & EVENTS

For those who know the Tower of London outside visiting hours, the fortress has a life of its own and a village-like quality, with its Governor, Chaplain, Doctor and Yeoman Warders and their families all living behind the walls that shut out the City beyond. In the past the resident community was much larger and more diverse, incorporating as it did a large garrison and a small army of officials of one sort or another.

The Yeoman Warders, definitely not to be referred to as 'Beef Eaters', represent the most obvious element of the community, but in historical terms are perhaps the least understood. First mentioned in documents dating from the early Tudor period, the Warders, or 'Waiters' as they were often referred to, formed and acted like a friendly society, sharing, by way of dividends, the rewards of their official and unofficial duties. The former included attending the gates, manning the night watch and guarding state prisoners; the latter, showing visitors the sights of the Tower. There were also monies from renting property in the Tower to innkeepers and others. Before dividends were issued, certain common expenses had to be met, among them the maintenance of the Warders' Hall, a building still standing (though much altered) immediately east of the Byward Tower.

The post of Yeoman Warder was handed down through the family or sold. This time-honoured practice was dealt a fatal blow in 1826, when the Duke of Wellington, as Constable of the Tower, ordered that in future the post was to be occupied by worthy non-commissioned officers of the Household Cavalry, Foot Guards and Infantry of the Line, solely on their regiment's recommendation. At the same time the process of revoking certain privileges began; one of the last to go was in April 1923, when the sale of picture postcards by Warders for their private profit was ended.

Until recent times the garrison formed the largest part of the Tower community. The Tower was garrisoned, in the modern sense, for the first time during the Commonwealth (1649–60). Since then the number of troops stationed in the castle has fluctuated, but probably reached its peak during the middle of the nineteenth century with the opening of the Waterloo Barracks, which was designed to accommodate 1,000 men.

As well as defending the Tower the garrison had a police role in and around London, and as late as January 1911 the 1st Battalion, Scots Guards, was called upon to assist the civil authorities during the famous Sidney Street siege in Stepney. In addition, the garrison always played, and still plays, a leading role in the ceremonial life of the Tower. This included guard changes, the famous Ceremony of the Keys and, until the removal of the small artillery contingent in 1924, responsibility for firing the Tower's gun salutes.

In April 1846 the Tower acquired its own police, numbering a sergeant and thirteen constables, provided by the Metropolitan force at a cost of £893 per annum. By 1900 the duty station was in the northern half of the Byward Tower, while the cells had been established in 2 Mint Street, a short distance to the north in the Outer Ward, in 1856. The sight of uniformed police officers strolling round the confines of the castle ended in January 1924 when, in an effort to achieve greater economy, the three sergeants and seven constables who by then made up the force were replaced by six Yeoman Warders who, together with their established colleagues, were issued with warrant cards for the purpose of arrest.

Since the fourteenth century, and probably before, the Tower had maintained a strip of ground between it and the City as a sort of buffer zone. The area, known as the Liberty, was jealously guarded by the Crown and was an endless source of conflict with the City, which had no civil or criminal jurisdiction over the people who lived there. Until the late nineteenth century the area was administered by a special local court with many of its officers being prominent Tower officials. In James II's reign three outlying areas in east London, the Minories, the Old Artillery Ground and the Wellclose, were formally added to the Liberty. The most potent symbols of Liberty authority, the court house and prison, were located in the Wellclose. For judicial purposes these ceased to exist on 25 June 1894 when the Liberty was formally dissolved. Not all traces of the Liberty disappeared, however. A few vestiges still remain, as evidenced by the Beating of the Bounds, a ceremony that takes place every third Ascension Day, when children from the Tower and choirboys from local churches perambulate the streets around the Tower beating the Liberty marker stones in order to remind everyone where the ancient boundary lies.

A Yeoman Warder photographed in State Dress uniform, *c.* 1870.

Thomas Faulkner appointed Yeoman Warder in 1889, and subsequently Chief Yeoman Ward in January 1903, seen here in State Dress uniform outside the Byward Tower in about 1890.

roup of Yeoman Warders in State Dress uniform in the Gun Park on the west side of the White Tower in the late
teenth century.

A stereoscopic postcard issued by James Davies Burton of a Yeoman Warder standing in front of Traitors' Gate in 1868 holding, for some unknown reason, a cat by the scruff of its neck! The main gates, which still exist, were installed in 1803 when the Thames flooded the basin beneath St Thomas's Tower. The smaller lattice gates above them, which also survive, are evidently earlier and were intended to allow small craft into the basin at high tide.

A Yeoman Warder wearing the normal Blue Undress uniform describes the site of the scaffold to tourists in the late nineteenth century.

This early photograph shows a group of Yeoman Warders near the Byward Tower. The Blue Undress uniform that they are wearing was introduced in November 1858 to a design by Messrs. Batt and Son of Edwards Street near Portman Square and replaced an earlier dress that originated from Tudor times.

A group of Yeoman Warders photographed in front of the arms of the Grand Storehouse in the late nineteenth century.

An early twentieth-century photograph of the Yeoman Gaoler outside his quarters on Tower Green with the celebrated processional axe.

Yeoman Warders wearing State Dress uniform outside the Chapel of St Peter ad Vincula in the 1920s, armed with partisans, which have been officially issued to them since the sixteenth century.

The newly installed Constable, General Sir Daniel Lysons, surrounded by the Officers and Yeoman Warders of the Tower in front of the Queen's House in 1890.

A photograph taken in 1896 of General Sir Daniel Lysons, the Constable of the Tower of London 1890–8.

A photograph also taken in 1896 of Lieutenant-General Bryan Milman, Resident Governor of the Tower of London 1874–1909.

A photograph of about 1921, showing, from left to right, A. Smoker, Chief Yeoman Warder; Major-General H. Pipon, Resident Governor; Field-Marshal Lord Methuen, Constable; and C. Gurney, Yeoman Gaoler.

A stereoscopic view of officers of the Scots Guards on the steps outside the Officers' Mess (now the Royal Fusiliers Museum) in the 1860s.

Men of the Scots Guards outside the Waterloo Barracks in the 1860s.

A photograph taken by James Davies Burton in 1868 showing Scots Guards parading in front of the Waterloo Barracks

Officers of the 1st Suffolk Regiment outside the Officers' Mess in 1895.

Detachment of the 1st Suffolk Regiment in formation at the Tower in 1895.

In 1898 the Ceremony of the Keys was uniquely performed during daylight hours for the benefit of the cameraman Benjamin Stone. Here the Chief Yeoman Warder, in his long scarlet coat and carrying the Queen's Keys, prepares to leave the Middle Tower with the escort party.

The party reaches the Byward Tower.

Having passed down Water Lane the party turn beneath the Bloody Tower.

The Keys and escort arrive at the old Main Guard, just north of the Bloody Tower.

Officer and guard present arms at the entrance to the old Main Guard.

A police sergeant on patrol in Water Lane during the closing years of the nineteenth century.

The Tower of London contingent of the Metropolitan Police Force photographed in front of the arms of the Grand Storehouse in the early twentieth century.

The Coast Brigade, Royal Artillery, with a
fire engine in Mint Street, *c.* 1870.

A military working party removing a
cannon bollard near the East Drawbridge,
c. 1870.

Army reservists at musketry drill in the Tower, 1896.

Artillery Volunteers on the Wharf during the early twentieth century.

An early twentieth-century postcard showing a guardsman on Brass Mount with the Royal Mint in the background.

Five Armouries foreman pictured in front of the arms of the Grand Storehouse in the 1880s.

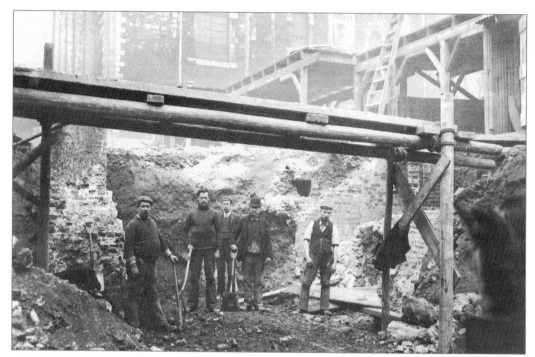

A photograph taken by Benjamin Stone in 1898 showing workmen on the site of the new Main Guard with the White Tower in the background.

Office of Works workmen unearthing ancient timbers during the re-excavation of part of Edward I's moat at the western entrance in 1937.

A photograph taken on 7 January 1928 showing damage to the Wharf in the immediate aftermath of an exceptionally high tide. As a consequence of this incident the existing flood barrier wall was erected on the Wharf.

Another photograph taken on 7 January 1928, showing flood waters in the western arm of the moat.

The historic ceremony known as Beating the Bounds, whereby the Resident Governor leads a procession about th
Liberties of the Tower to reaffirm the Crown's authority over the strip of ground beyond the moat, probably date
back to 1582 when the Lieutenant organised a perambulation. On that occasion he ordered the inhabitants of th
locality to bring certain children aged twelve to fourteen who were given a sheaf arrow 'for a remembrance th
they had made their entry in right of the Crown'. Here we see the participants gathered at the Tower before the
perambulation during the 1930s.

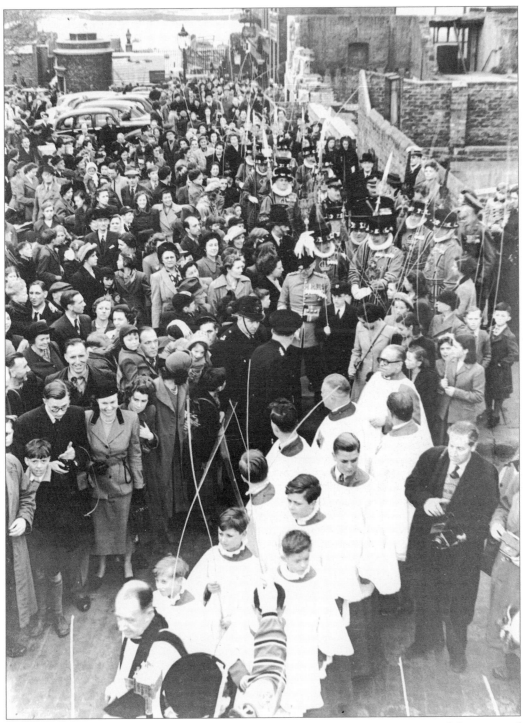

With crowds of onlookers on side and bomb-damaged sites on the other, a procession of choirmen and boys led by the Resident Governor and other officials is seen here during the 1950s making its way up Tower Hill during the Beating of the Bounds.

Charles ffoulkes, Curator of the Armouries, reads an address in front of the Main Guard on 30 January 1930 during the unveiling of a tablet to commemorate the Rev. Alexander John Forsyth, inventor of the percussion lock.

On 23 July 1934 an artificial beach was officially opened on the foreshore of the Tower of London for the benefit of the underprivileged residents of East London. It proved to be immensely popular, as this photograph taken in the aftermath of the Second World War demonstrates. Despite growing concerns about the hazards of bathing in the polluted waters of the Thames, the beach continued in use until the 1960s.

Yeoman Warder H.T. Jones, who joined the Body of Yeoman Warders in 1946 and retired from active duty in 1970, is pictured here with 'Charlie', one of the famous Tower ravens.

A timeless act! This photograph, taken in about 1950, shows a Yeoman Warder in the Warders' Hall adjusting a clock which the Warders purchased on 23 November 1694 for the sum of £9, and have maintained ever since.

ACKNOWLEDGEMENTS

I should like to record my particular thanks to Peter Hammond, former Deputy Master of the Royal Armouries, for reading the text and making various amendments and offering useful advice. Cliff Birtchnell clambered over roofs, and dodged cars and tourists alike, to photograph contemporary equivalents of many of the historic views. Apart from anything else his results highlight the difference between the work of a professional photographer and the efforts of a rank amateur like myself.

The official photographic record of the Tower of London, begun by the Office of Works at the start of this century, and enlarged and handed down via the Ministry of Public Buildings and Works and the Department of the Environment, is now dispersed. Generally speaking, the earlier part of the collection, comprising photographs taken before about 1950, is with the Royal Commission on Historic Monuments (England) and was in the process of being re-catalogued at the time the research for this book was undertaken. Later photographs, again generally speaking, are with the Royal Armouries and the Historic Royal Palaces Agency. There is, however, a certain amount of duplication in all three collections. In addition English Heritage retains a large number of related photographs (some of negatives now lost or unlocated) dating to before 1984. Many carry contemporary captions and thus provide an indispensable index to the material in the other three collections.

Against that complicated backdrop I have tried to apportion copyright on the best information available. If errors have been made I apologise for them now. Any such omissions will be corrected in subsequent editions.

T   said, the photographs reproduced here
of the following: Body of Yeoman Warders, pp. 96 top, 105, 106 bottom, 107, 116 top, 121, 124-5; Guildhall Library, Corporation of London, pp. 26, 31, 38 top, 46 top, 76 bottom, 103 top, 114 top; Historic Royal Palaces pp. 78, 94 bottom, 96 bottom; B.E.C. Howarth-Loomes, pp. 12, 16 top, 44, 61 top, 102; Howard Ricketts, pp. 15 bottom, 32, 35 top, 40, 43 top, 51 top, 63–5 top, 66-71 top, 99, 115: Imperial war Museum, pp. 81, 83, 94 top; Museum of London, p. 92 bottom; National Portrait Gallery, p. 29 top; Royal Armouries, pp. 2, 5, 11, 13, 14, 15 top, 16 bottom, 17, 19, 20-8, 29 bottom, 30, 33-4, 35 bottom, 36, 37 top, 38 bottom, 39, 41-2, 43 bottom, 45, 46 bottom, 47-9, 50 bottom, 51 bottom, 53-5, 56 bottom, 60 bottom, 61 bottom, 62, 71 bottom, 73-6 top, 77, 82, 84- 92 top, 104, 106 top, 108, 109 bottom, 110-13, 1114 bottom, 116-20, 123; Royal Commission on Historic Monuments (England), p. 18; Royal Engineers Museum, p. 6; Royal Institute of British Architects, pp. 7-8; C. Wilkinson, p. 56 top.

Other titles published by The History Press

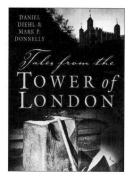

Tales from the Tower of London
DANIEL DIEHL & MARK P. DONNELLY

A history of the building itself, told through the stories of the people, royal and common, good and bad, heroes and villains, who lived and died there. This book presents a microcosm of human experience, from love and death to greed and betrayal, all played out against romantic period settings ranging from medieval knights to the days of WWII.

978-0-7509-3497-8

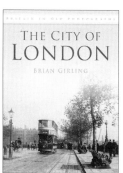

The City of London In Old Photographs
BRIAN GIRLING

This book paints the fascinating picture of the events and people which helped shaped the city we know so well today, including the building and wartime destruction of some of its characteristic features. Focusing on the famous heart of London, most of the images date from the Edwardian period and slightly after, when London was arguably the greatest city in the world.

978-0-7524-4935-7

The Great Fire of London
STEPHEN PORTER

The Great Fire of London in 1666 was the greatest catastrophe of its kind in Western Europe. In this comprehensive study Stephen Porter examines the background to 1666, and places the fire firmly in context, revealing not only its impact on London's fabric, but also its implications for town planning, building styles and fire precautions both in the capital and provincial towns.

978-0-7524-5025-4

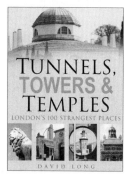

Tunnels, Towers & Temples: London's 100 Strangest Place
David Long

Tunnels, Towers & Temples takes a sideways look at London, revealing the hidden stories, curious histories and sometimes comic associations behind dozens of often quite familiar places. Through their stories, the author reveals a strange side of London most people never come to know. This book is the best possible start for anyone who wishes to get off the beaten track and under the skin of the hidden city that is modern-day London.

978-0-7509-4509-7

Visit our website and discover thousands of other History Press books.

www.thehistorypress.co.uk